15HD

D1214209

BOOKWORMS

What's Inside Me?
My Stomach

¿Qué hay dentro de mí?
El estómago

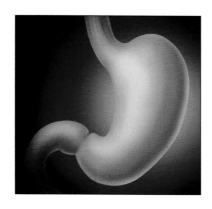

Dana Meachen Rau

Marshall Cavendish
Benchmark
New York

My Stomach

El estómago

TEETH
DIENTES

MOUTH
BOCA

TONGUE
LENGUA

ESOPHAGUS
ESÓFAGO

STOMACH
ESTÓMAGO

LARGE
INTESTINE

INTESTINO
GRUESO

SMALL
INTESTINE

INTESTINO
DELGADO

RECTUM
RECTO

3

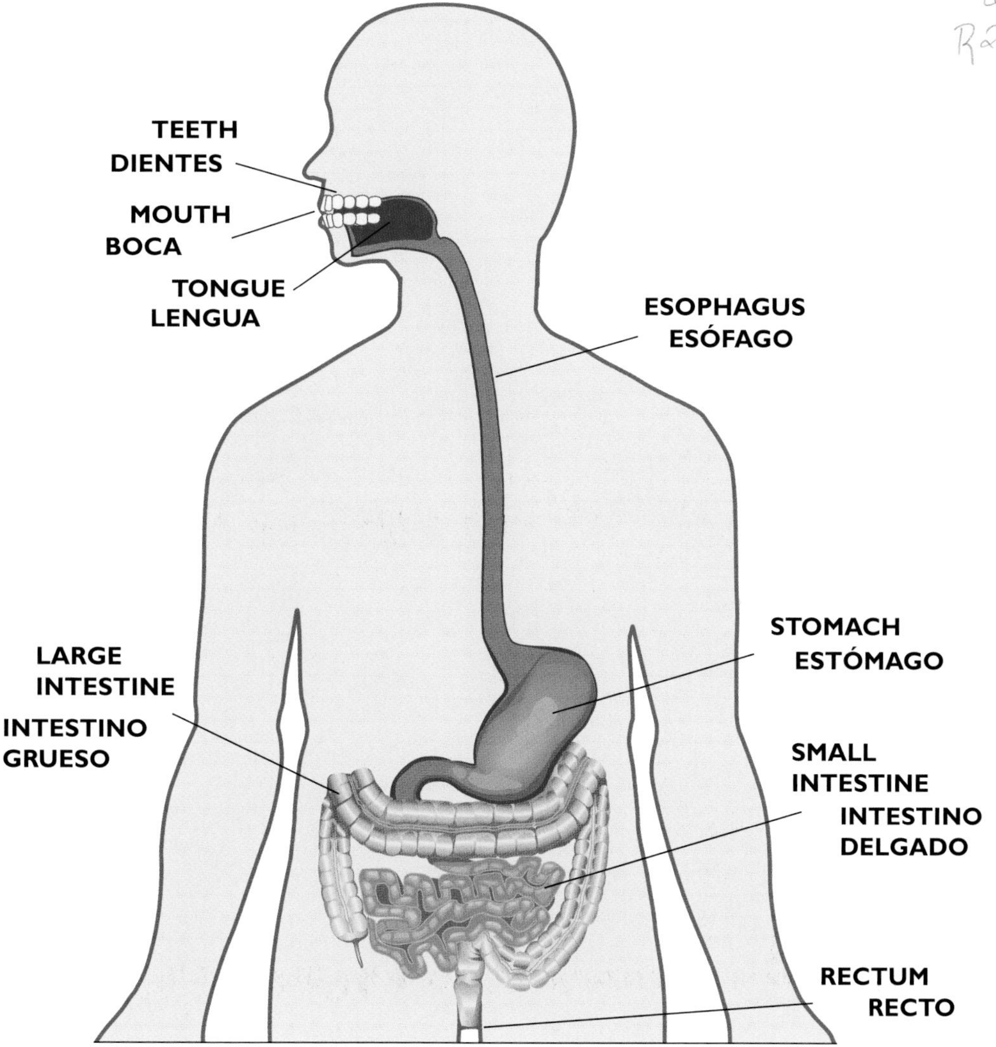

4

What did you bring for lunch today? Peanut butter on wheat bread is yummy. Carrots are crunchy. Milk is a healthy drink.

❖

¿Qué trajiste hoy de merienda? El pan integral con mantequilla de maní siempre es rico. Las zanahorias están crujientes. La leche es una bebida saludable.

Your body needs food to grow. Food gives your body *energy*.

❖

Tu cuerpo necesita comida para crecer. La comida te da *energía*.

Food keeps you strong and healthy.

Los alimentos te mantienen el cuerpo fuerte
y sano.

You eat food every day. It goes into your mouth. *Waste* from your food comes out of your body when you go to the bathroom.

Te alimentas todos los días. La comida entra por la boca. Los *residuos* de la comida que comes salen de tu cuerpo cuando vas al baño.

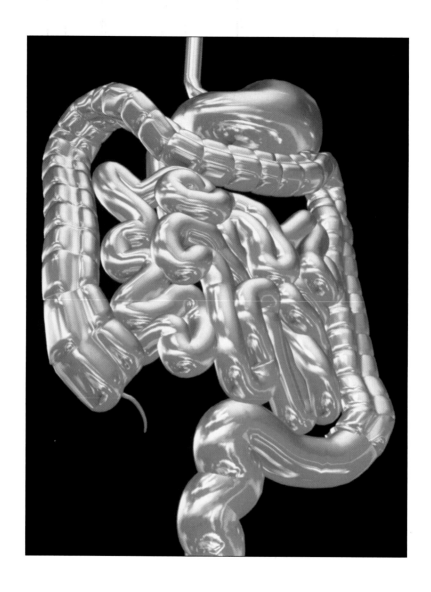

But what happens to the food while it is inside you?

Food travels a long path through your body. This path is called the *digestive system*.

Pero, ¿qué pasa con la comida mientras está dentro de tu cuerpo?

La comida hace un largo viaje por tu cuerpo recorriendo el *sistema digestivo*.

Your stomach is an important part of your digestive system. It turns food into *nutrients*. Nutrients are used by all parts of your body.

El estómago es una parte importante del sistema digestivo. Convierte la comida en *nutrientes* que las diferentes partes de tu cuerpo usan.

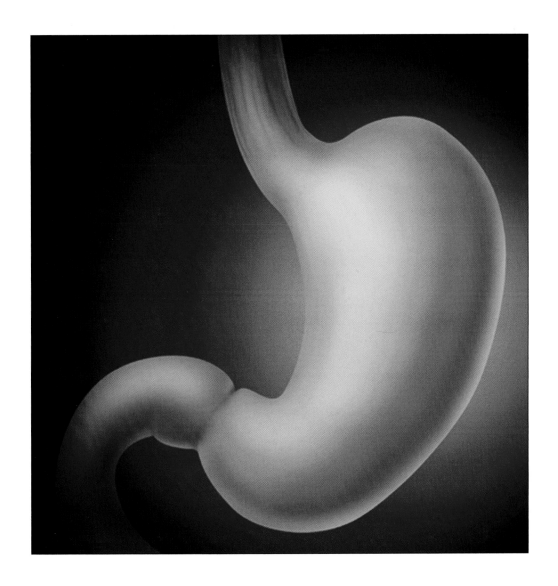

13

14

You put food in your mouth. Your teeth chew your food. *Saliva*, or spit, mixes with food and makes it soft.

Next, you *swallow*. Your tongue pushes the food to the back of your throat.

Pones comida en tu boca, los dientes la mastican, y la *saliva* mezcla la comida y la ablanda.

Luego, *tragas*. Tu lengua empuja la comida hacia tu garganta.

The food travels down a tube called the *esophagus*. The tube leads into your stomach.

Your stomach is like a bag.
It holds the food.

La comida baja por un tubo llamado *esófago*. Este tubo lleva la comida al estómago.

El estómago es como una bolsa que contiene la comida.

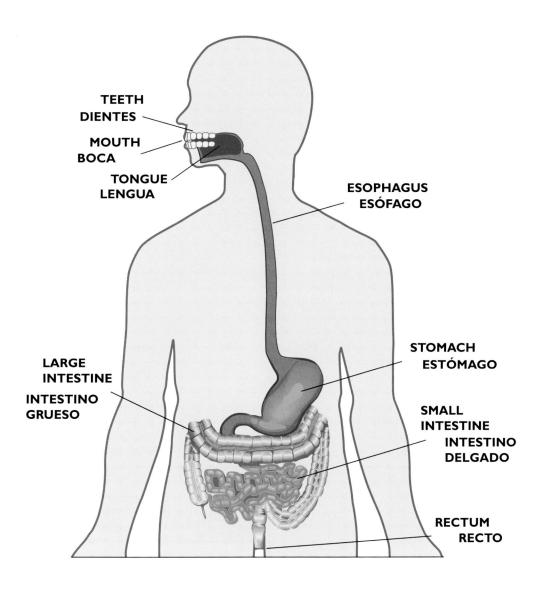

TEETH
DIENTES

MOUTH
BOCA

TONGUE
LENGUA

ESOPHAGUS
ESÓFAGO

STOMACH
ESTÓMAGO

LARGE
INTESTINE
INTESTINO
GRUESO

SMALL
INTESTINE
INTESTINO
DELGADO

RECTUM
RECTO

17

The inside of your stomach is bumpy. Your stomach stretches bigger and bigger as you eat more food.

You feel full when you have a lot of food in your stomach.

El interior del estómago es arrugado. Mientras más comes, más se agranda tu estómago.

Estás lleno o llena cuando hay mucha comida en tu estómago.

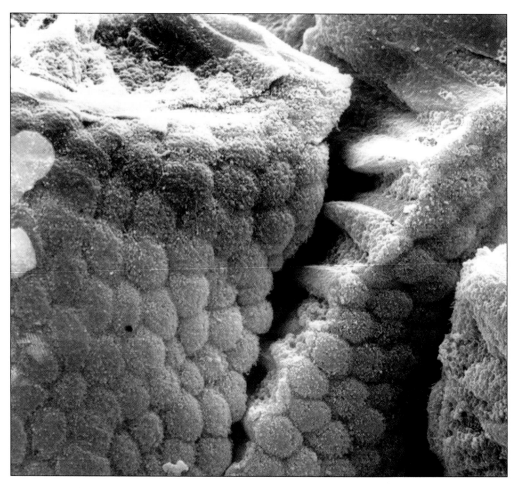

Inside the stomach

❖

El estómago por dentro

Your stomach is very strong. It moves around to mush up food into small pieces. Juices in your stomach make the food very soft.

The food is filled with nutrients. It becomes thick and soupy.

El estómago es muy fuerte. Se mueve para deshacer la comida en pedacitos, mientras que los jugos del estómago la ablandan.

La comida, que está llena de nutrientes, se convierte en una sopa espesa.

Food stays in your stomach for about three hours. Then your stomach pushes the food into another tube. It is called the *small intestine*.

The small intestine is very long and thin. It winds around inside your body.

La comida se queda en tu estómago por unas tres horas. Luego, el estómago la empuja por otro tubo llamado *intestino delgado*.

El intestino delgado es muy largo y fino. Se enrolla dentro de tu cuerpo.

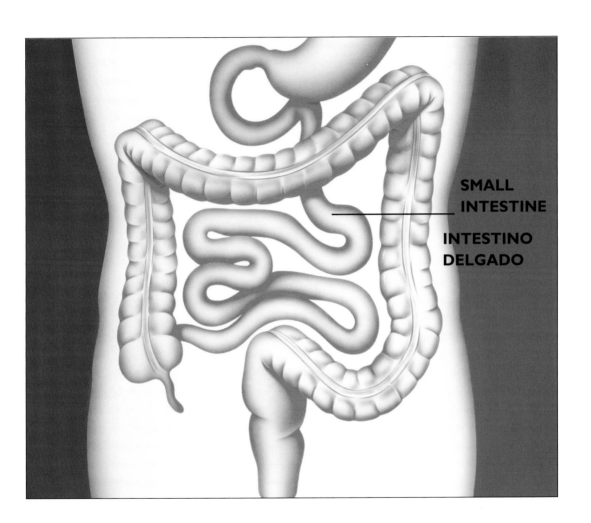

SMALL INTESTINE

INTESTINO DELGADO

23

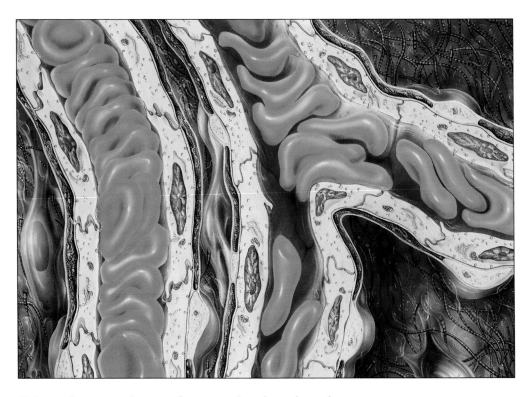

Blood traveling through the body

❖

La sangre viaja por el cuerpo

From the small intestine, the nutrients go into your blood.

Blood travels all around your body. It carries the nutrients to parts of your body that need them.

❖

Los nutrientes van del intestino delgado a la sangre.

La sangre viaja por todo el cuerpo. Lleva nutrientes a las partes del cuerpo que los necesitan.

The small intestine leads to another tube. It is called the *large intestine*.

The large intestine gets rid of the food your body does not need. Waste travels through the large intestine to your *rectum*. Then the waste leaves your body through an opening.

El intestino delgado termina en otro tubo llamado *intestino grueso*.

El intestino grueso se deshace de la comida que tu cuerpo no necesita. Los residuos viajan por el intestino grueso hacia el *recto*. Luego, los residuos dejan tu cuerpo por una abertura.

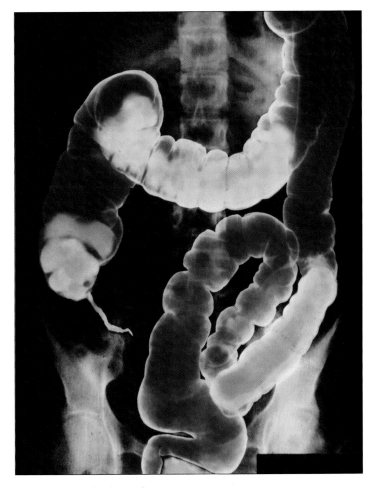

X-ray of the large intestine

❖

Rayos X del intestino grueso

You need to eat good food every day.

❖

Necesitas comer alimentos buenos todos los días.

Healthy food gives you a healthy body.

La comida saludable hace que tu cuerpo esté sano.

Challenge Words

digestive system The path food travels through your body.

energy What your body needs to be active.

esophagus The tube that leads from your mouth to your stomach.

large intestine The tube that leads from your small intestine to your rectum.

nutrients The parts of food your body needs to stay healthy.

rectum The end of your large intestine.

saliva The watery juice in your mouth that makes food soft.

small intestine The long tube that sends nutrients into the blood.

swallow To move food from your mouth into your esophagus.

waste The parts of food your body does not need.

Palabras avanzadas

energía Lo que el cuerpo necesita para estar activo.

esófago El tubo que conecta la boca con el estómago.

intestino delgado El tubo largo que lleva los nutrientes a la sangre.

intestino grueso El tubo que conecta el intestino delgado con el recto.

nutrientes Las sustancias de la comida que el cuerpo necesita para mantenerse sano.

recto Donde termina el intestino grueso.

residuo La parte de la comida que el cuerpo no necesita.

saliva La sustancia en tu boca que ablanda la comida.

sistema digestivo El conjunto de órganos por donde viaja la comida.

tragar Mover la comida de la boca al esófago.

Index

Índice

With thanks to Nanci Vargus, Ed.D.
and Beth Walker Gambro, reading consultants

Marshall Cavendish Benchmark
99 White Plains Road
Tarrytown, New York 10591-9001
www.marshallcavendish.us

Library of Congress Cataloging-in-Publication Data

Rau, Dana Meachen, 1971–
[My stomach. Spanish & English]
My stomach = El estómago / Dana Meachen Rau. — Bilingual ed.
p. cm. — (Bookworms. What's inside me? = ¿Qué hay dentro de mí?)
Includes index.
ISBN-13: 978-0-7614-2485-7 (bilingual edition)
ISBN-10: 0-7614-2485-7 (bilingual edition)
ISBN-13: 978-0-7614-2407-9 (Spanish edition)
ISBN-10: 0-7614-1782-6 (English edition)
1. Stomach—Juvenile literature. 2. Gastrointestinal system—Juvenile literature.
3. Digestion—Juvenile literature. I. Title. II. Title: El estómago. III. Series: Rau, Dana Meachen, 1971–
Bookworms. What's inside me? (Spanish & English)

QP151.R3818 2006b
612.3—dc22
2006016715

Spanish Translation and Text Composition by Victory Productions, Inc.
www.victoryprd.com

Photo Research by Anne Burns Images

Cover Photo by Corbis: Royalty Free

The photographs in this book are used with permission and through the courtesy of:
Custom Medical Stock Photo: pp. 1, 13, 20. Jay Mallin: p. 2. Corbis: p. 4 Charles Gupton; p. 6 Bob Winsett;
p. 7 David H. Wells; p. 9 Norbert Schaefer; p. 14 Richard Gross; p. 18 Christoph Wilhelm;
p. 28 LWA-Sharie Kennedy; p. 28 Ed Bock. Photo Researchers: p. 10 Alfred Pasieka; p. 23 John Bavosi;
p. 24 Medical Art Service; p. 27 CNRI.

Series design by Becky Terhune

Printed in Malaysia
1 3 5 6 4 2